by E. C. Andrews

Minneapolis, Minnesota

Credits
Images are courtesy of Shutterstock.com. With thanks to Getty Images, Thinkstock Photo, and iStockphoto. Recurring – schab, nabil refaat, Maquiladora, A.Aruno. Cover – hvostik, orifec_a31. 4–5 – Aaronejbull87, Lindsey Lu. 6–7 – DiveSpin.Com, Rich Carey. 8–9 – Papzi555, Andrea Izzotti. 10–11 – Andrea Izzotti, Fata Morgana by Andrew Marriott. 12–13 – Tunatura. 14–15 – Andrea Izzotti, DJ Mattaar. 16–17 – JirkaVo, Rich Carey. 18–19 – Adam Leaders, Jason LSL. 20–21 – Aaronejbull87, Chainarong Phrammanee. 22–23 – Aaronejbull87, wildestanimal.

Bearport Publishing Company Product Development Team
President: Jen Jenson; Director of Product Development: Spencer Brinker; Managing Editor: Allison Juda; Associate Editor: Naomi Reich; Associate Editor: Tiana Tran; Art Director: Colin O'Dea; Designer: Kim Jones; Designer: Kayla Eggert; Product Development Assistant: Owen Hamlin

Library of Congress Cataloging-in-Publication Data is available at www.loc.gov or upon request from the publisher.

ISBN: 979-8-89232-064-1 (hardcover)
ISBN: 979-8-89232-538-7 (paperback)
ISBN: 979-8-89232-197-6 (ebook)

© 2025 BookLife Publishing
This edition is published by arrangement with BookLife Publishing.

North American adaptations © 2025 Bearport Publishing Company. All rights reserved. No part of this publication may be reproduced in whole or in part, stored in any retrieval system, or transmitted in any form or by any means, electronic, mechanical, photocopying, recording, or otherwise, without written permission from the publisher. Bearport Publishing is a division of Chrysalis Education Group.

For more information, write to Bearport Publishing, 5357 Penn Avenue South, Minneapolis, MN 55419.

CONTENTS

The Whale Shark.............4
Diet........................6
Mouth 8
Nose 10
Eyes 12
Skin....................... 14
Skeleton 16
Fins....................... 18
Tail 20
Life Cycle 22
Glossary 24
Index......................24

THE WHALE SHARK

There are more than 500 different kinds of sharks. Whale sharks are the biggest of them all!

Whale sharks got their name in part because they are so large. They can grow to be about 60 feet (18 m). That's longer than a school bus!

DIET

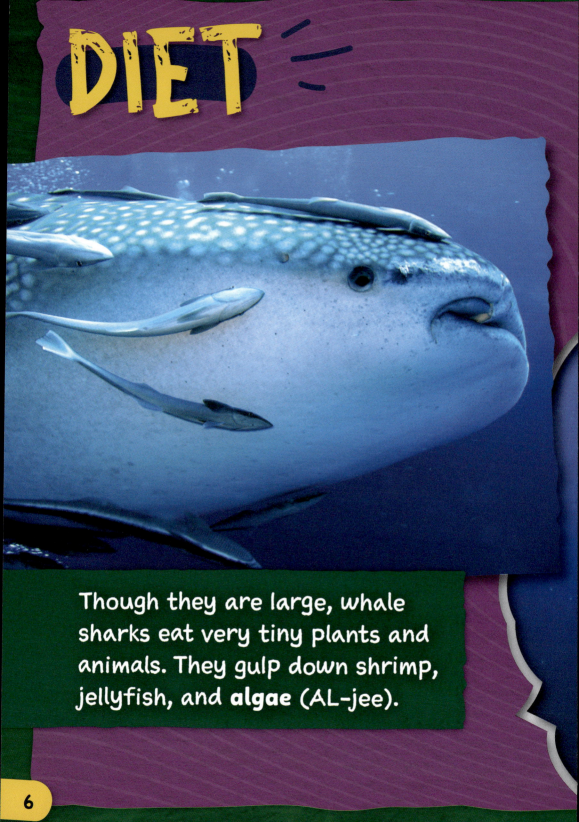

Though they are large, whale sharks eat very tiny plants and animals. They gulp down shrimp, jellyfish, and **algae** (AL-jee).

For most of the year, whale sharks eat a lot. Then, they go for about four months without eating. During this time, they swim across the open ocean.

MOUTH

Whale sharks have many small teeth in their large mouths. However, they do not use these teeth for eating.

These huge sharks are **filter feeders**. They open their mouths and swim forward. Then, they push the water out and swallow only the food.

NOSE

A whale shark's **nostrils** are just above the top part of its mouth. The large animal has a very good sense of smell.

NOSTRIL

The shark uses its sense of smell to sniff out food.

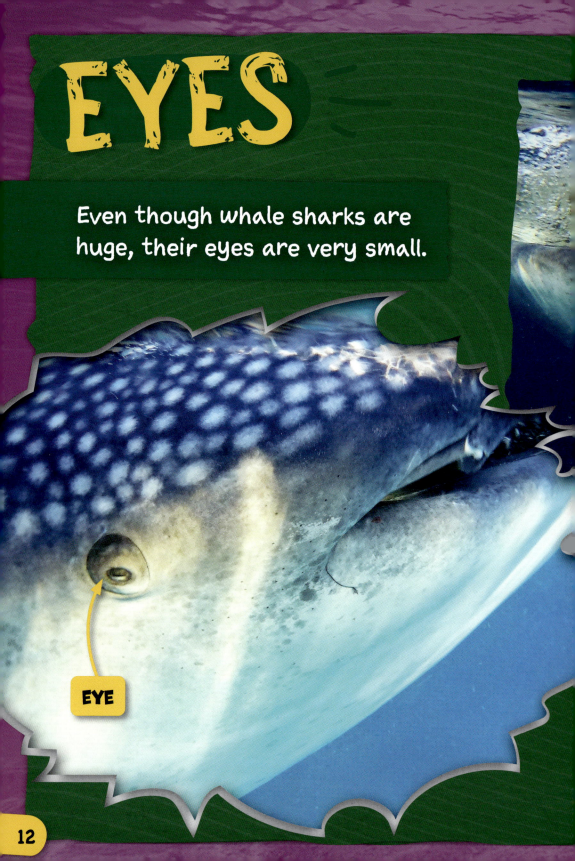

EYES

Even though whale sharks are huge, their eyes are very small.

EYE

Whale sharks do not have eyelids. Instead, hundreds of little **scales** cover their eyeballs. This keeps things from harming their eyes.

SKIN

The shark's skin also has scales. These tiny toothlike scales feel very rough.

Whale sharks are covered in spots and stripes. You can tell the sharks apart from one another because they each have different markings.

SKELETON

Sharks do not have bones. Their skeletons are made of **cartilage**. Cartilage is softer and more bendy than bone.

Cartilage is lighter than bone, too. This makes it easier for whale sharks to float.

FINS

A whale shark has a few kinds of fins. Each helps the shark do different things.

18

The dorsal fin on its back keeps the whale shark from rolling over. Pectoral (PEK-tur-uhl) fins stick out from the sides of its body. They help the shark turn.

TAIL

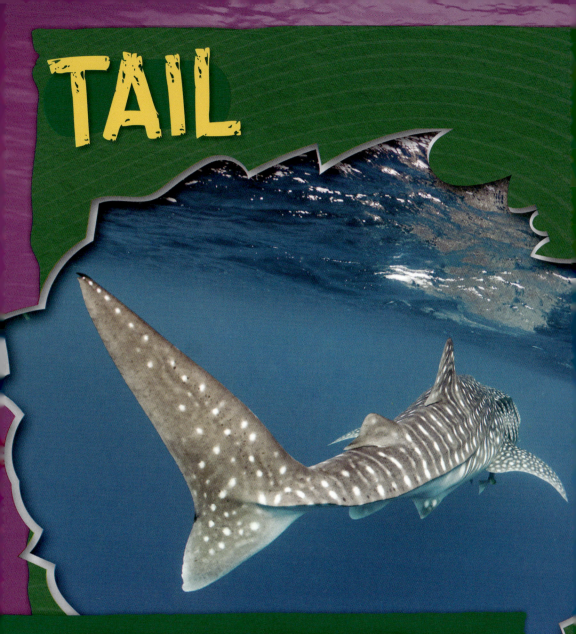

Whale sharks use their tail fins and the back part of their bodies to swim. They move these parts from side to side. This pushes them forward.

Because of their size, whale sharks are slow swimmers. Moving slowly helps them use less **energy**.

LIFE CYCLE

Baby whale sharks are called pups. They **hatch** from eggs inside their mother's body. A mother whale shark can have about 300 pups at once.

These huge animals usually live for about 70 years. However, some whale sharks have lived to be 150 years old!

GLOSSARY

algae tiny plantlike living things that grow in water

cartilage the strong, rubbery stuff that makes up a shark's skeleton

energy the power needed by all living things to grow and stay alive

filter feeders animals that take food from water in order to eat

hatch to come out of an egg

nostrils two openings in a nose used for smelling

scales small, hard pieces that form a shark's skin

INDEX

cartilage 16–17
eggs 22
fins 18–20
food 9, 11
nostrils 10
pups 22
scales 13–14
spots 15
teeth 8, 14